Nature Trails
Captured in Color

by Mary Calvert

To Janice Ann
and Mary Ann with all good wishes
from the authors
Mary Calvert
Sept 30, 1986

Library of Congress No. 83-82646
Copyright 1982 by Mary Calvert

ISBN No. 0-9609914-2-5

Printed by Twin City Printery
Lewiston, Maine

Many thanks to:

    My husband Francis for the many hours of editing and bending over a slide viewer with a magnifying glass to examine pictures. His advice, help and encouragement were invaluable.

    Florence Heyl for the use of her column "You Can Find It Wild" which appears in *The Boothbay Register, The Wiscasset Newspaper,* and *The Lincoln County News.*

    Elizabeth Hamilton Hartsgrove for the use of her poem "Trees" from her book *Maine Heritage.*

    Selections from *The Edge of the Sea* by Rachel Carson, copyright © 1955 by Rachel L. Carson, are reprinted by permission of Houghton Mifflin Company.

    Excerpts from *Under the Sea Wind* by Rachel L. Carson, copyright © 1941 by Rachel L. Carson, renewed 1969 by Roger Christie, are reprinted by permission of Oxford University Press, Inc.

*Dedicated with much love
to my daughters
Jeannette and Anita
who learned Nature's ways
hiking through the wilderness
with their Maine grandfather*

Mary Calvert

Nature's Wonderland can be found in all its glory in the State of Maine. Its huge wooded northland — its network of lakes and streams — its Atlantic shores washed continuously with salt spray — all provide a perfect setting for wild flowers, forests, and animal and bird life.

Carrabassett Ice

Enjoying our natural heritage is a tradition which has come down to us from the red man. Their language was descriptive, containing many terms taken from nature. Favorite names for Indian girls were Little Flower, Red Feather or Pink Cloud, while boys' names were more indicative of swiftness or strength such as Brown Deer, Mighty Moose, Little Fawn or Red Eagle.

Indians divided the year into sections which they called "moons," and gave them picturesque names descriptive of happenings at that particular time. Early winter was the Moon of Crackling Trees. Frost, the first snows and sharp winds caused the branches to break and fall to the ground making crackling noises which broke the silence of the forest. These sounds were the signal for the braves to hunt and for the squaws to prepare stores of corn for the coming moon.

The Moon of the Deep Snows was the cruelest of the moons. Cold and dwindling food supplies caused much anxiety. Canoes were stored and snowshoes repaired to become the Indians' means of transportation through the snow-covered forests.

But at last when the ice began to melt, the Indians could look forward to the Moon of the Flowers which would spread joy in the wigwams of the village, as it does now in our hearts when we go out into the mellow spring air and catch a glimpse of the first wild flower of the new season.

Next page: Carrabassett "Ice-out"

Spring, wonderful capricious spring, so welcome after the long, cold days of winter and that last unexpected blizzard. Streams and brooks are now filled to overflowing, and the banks are lost to view under the swollen waters of the spring freshets.

Lobster Stream, locally called Lobster Trip, is the outlet of Lobster Lake emptying into the West Branch of the Penobscot River — that is, most of the time. Due to the vagaries of water level and currents, it can become an inlet with the water flowing from the river into the lake. Hence a "trip" was built many years ago to keep the water and the log drives on the proper course. Some years ago, before the log drives ended, a fisherman forgot to close the log trip behind him and, before he reached the lake, found to his chagrin that he was being closely followed by the entire spring drive of logs.

Waterfalls become raging torrents. Moxie Stream is the outlet of Moxie Pond, and it tumbles downhill for about eight miles of its winding and twisting course over a series of cascades.

Moxie Falls, with a sheer drop of ninety-six feet, is a beautiful woodland waterfall situated on the stream about a half mile before it joins the Kennebec River not far above the Forks.

Deer trot out into the open fields at the edge of the woods hunting for new, tender grass to eat as a welcome change from the dry, cold reindeer moss which has been their mainstay all winter.

But — who is that?

Sandy Stream, near Middle Carry Pond, photographed from the Arnold Trail.

The mighty moose makes his ponderous way to the nearest shallow pond to wade and feed on the grasses and lily pads now springing up.

Small animals sense that winter is almost over. According to an old legend, the groundhog pokes his head above ground on February 2 and, if he sees his shadow, is frightened back into his burrow for another six weeks.

But if he doesn't see his shadow, he ventures out to meet his friends. After all, isn't spring the time for love? Tra la, tra la!

Fiddleheads

The cycle of the seasons has begun. The winter woods which looked brown and lifeless have begun to stir and come to life. Here and there, if we look carefully, we can find a patch of green making its way upward through last fall's dead leaves.

The loveliness of spring! It is an awakening, a renewal of hope, a touch of warmth in the air, the soft, slanting rays of the sun filtering through the trees after a shower. It is May, the Indians' "Moon of the Flowers."

It is the sight of the first wild flower of the season, perhaps the sweet-scented trailing arbutus or mayflower. Drop to your knees and drink in its delicate coloring and elusive perfume, as it is tiny and sometimes hidden under its shiny green leaves. Enjoy it and leave, taking it along in your memory or on film as it is becoming very rare and resists transplanting.

This flower grows on a creeping evergreen plant which has a woody stem. The buds are formed earlier in the winter or even late fall, and then protected by the leaves until spring. There are five petals joined at the base to form a short tube which expands to form the blossom.

They grow abundantly in the vicinity of Plymouth, and it was said to be the first flower to greet the Pilgrims after that fearful first winter. John Greenleaf Whittier wrote a poem about the first mayflower sighting in the New World.

The Mayflowers
Sad Mayflower! Watched by winter stars,
And nursed by winter gales,
With petals of the sleeted spars
And leaves of frozen sails!
What had she in those dreary hours,
Within her ice-rimmed bay,
In common with the wild-wood flowers,
The first sweet smiles of May!
Yet, "God be praised!" the Pilgrim said,
Who saw the blossoms peer
Above the brown leaves, dry and dead,
"Behold our Mayflower here!"
"God wills it" here our rest shall be,
Our years of wandering o'er,
For us the Mayflower of the sea
Shall spread her sails no more.

Then Whittier gives us the message of hope and rebirth inherent in the coming of spring.

"O sacred flower of faith and hope,
As sweetly now as then,
Ye bloom on many a birchen slope,
In many a pine dark glen.
But warmer suns erelong shall bring
To life the frozen sod;
And, through dead leaves of hope, shall spring
Afresh the flowers of God!

The nature lover or photographer, and they are often one and the same, who wishes to follow the fascinating wild flower trail must be ready very early in the spring to put on rubber boots and a warm jacket as April showers bring the slumbering and apparently dead forest to life once again. The earliest flowers must push aside brown leaves from the preceding autumn and make use of the sun's rays before the tree leaves come out.

The ethereal goldthread is only 3 to 5 inches in height with 5 to 7 waxen white sepals and a yellow center. The flower is not more than three quarters of an inch wide, and it grows on the end of a leafless stalk.

Its name derives from its golden, threadlike rhyzome which produces a yellow dye with medicinal properties. Indians used it for canker sores, sore throat and for teething babies.

I photographed this little flower in the woods surrounding Kidney Pond in Baxter State Park in a light rain.

Goldthread in a Woodland Setting

Marsh Marigolds

While water still stands in the marshy parts of intervales, this pretty flower springs up in large patches to make a golden carpet on the edges of bogs and streams. Since this plant grows with its feet in the water, the photographer often ends up that way too.

They are sometimes called cowslips and have from five to nine shiny bright yellow petals. Although much larger than buttercups, marsh marigolds are members of that family and the resemblance is easy to see.

Bluets and Violets

Bluets grow profusely in New England, and although we think of them as spring flowers, they are seen as late as July. They often cover large areas of meadow or lawn. The small enamel-like blossoms grow so thickly that a large patch presents a picture of solid white or light blue.

In this picture bluets are growing among blue violets, showing how nature sometimes groups flowers in pleasing arrangements.

Bluets or Quaker Ladies

May in the Maine countryside means bluets. Myriads of these dainty pale blue or white flowers with a bright yellow center grow in patches in meadows or even lawns. They are also called Quaker Ladies.

Don't ignore this flower because it is tiny. Like many miniatures, it is a real beauty.

Mayapple or Mandrake

Two great umbrella-like leaves completely hide the lovely waxen white blossom of the mayapple. One should kneel to get a good look. They are not common but will spread quite rapidly when in a woodsy location they like. My three transplanted mayapples have multiplied nicely in a few years.

The name mayapple is derived from the fact that after the flower has faded, it is replaced by a fruit shaped like a small apple.

Great Solomon's Seal

The pale green bell-shaped blossoms of the great Solomon's seal hang from the long curving stem of this plant. Often four feet high, they grow in rich woods or on riverbanks. I photographed this one at Pownalborough Courthouse in Dresden where they grow around the front steps of the building.

Blue Meadow Violet

Whose heart has not been gladdened by the sight of a clump of purplish-blue violets with their distinctive heart-shaped leaves, or even the sight of one in its bed of moss.

One of our loveliest harbingers of spring, it has been a favorite of poet and naturalist alike. Its pure color and heart-shaped leaves have graced many a Valentine, as it seems perfectly suited to messages of love.

Toulouse, France is noted for its violets and the perfume made from them. An unknown poet of the nineteenth century wrote:

> *Purple Violets lurk,*
> *With all the lovely children of the shade.*

Shakespeare adds his words of tribute:

> *. . . sweeter than the lids of Juno's eyes*
> *Or Cytherea's breath, . . .*

Our Maine hillsides are well covered with violets in May and early June.

Upon the Water's velvet edge, the purple violet breathes delight —
Close nestled to the grassy sedge.

Written by an unknown Victorian poet

The downy yellow violet with petals so soft they appear as though cut from the softest of velvets.

My downy yellows bloom the first week in June, which might be a little late as they are on the edge of a shady wooded area. The plant is from eight to sixteen inches tall, and the stem and leaves are covered with downy soft hairs, hence the name.

Bloodroot Buds

In early spring, the tightly curled up leaf of the bloodroot pushes its way up through the earth, then through a layer of last fall's brown leaves, bearing its tightly shielded burden, a young and erect flower bud. When the leaf unfurls, we are treated to a view of a snowy white blossom with from six to twelve petals encircling a golden center. These flowers like to grow on partially shaded slopes or rich woodlands. The red juice which oozes from the cut stem gave the flower its name and was highly prized by the Indians who used it for painting their faces and tomahawks for the warpath.

Once I was lucky enough to come across a bloodroot-carpeted hillside in a friend's woods — what a beautiful sight!

Wild ginger is a challenge to photograph. As you can see, it grows in a topsy-turvy fashion with the dark red blossom at the base of the plant resting right on the ground. (You can guess my undignified position when taking the picture.)

   To find the trout lily, otherwise known as adder's-tongue or cowslip, we direct our steps toward a small hollow in a meadow which is watered by a brook or spring. There where the sunlight filters its way through the still leafless branches, we often find myriads of these charming pale yellow lilies, each hanging downward from its slender curving stem.

The jack-in-the-pulpit is a striking and exotic spring flower. The spathe, often striped, surrounds and curls over the club-like spike which reminded someone of a tiny preacher in his pulpit, thus the name.

The month of May brings forth the pale pink or white blossoms of the rue anemone or wind flower. The last is a very appropriate name as they wave about on their slender stems in the slightest breeze, to the despair of shutterbugs.

Hepatica Americana

The hepatica is one of my favorite spring flowers as it bursts forth from the seemingly dormant floor of the woods very early. It is always a thrilling surprise to see the beautiful small blossoms in a bed of brown leaves which they have had to push aside to emerge.

They vary in color from white through various tones of pink and lavender. Leaves do not appear until after the flower has faded. The leaves are large and liver shaped, giving rise to the flower's other name, liverwort. Indians and early settlers used it for liver ailments!

The beautiful petal-like sepals furnish the color in this blossom. Another distinctive feature is the fuzz along the whole length of the stem, almost like a tiny fur coat protecting the fragile looking plant from the early spring cold and sometimes even a sprinkle of snow.

Large Flowering Trillium — Lily Family

Everything comes in threes on a trillium. There are three rather large leaves. Rising from the center of the leaves is a short stem carrying a flower with three long, pointed white petals, three green sepals, a three-part pistil and six stamens.

This trillium is common in Ohio and New York State, but in Maine is only found growing naturally in Franklin County. However, it may be transplanted if treated with care, and I have a few doing well on a wooded slope.

The Painted Trillium

In contrast to the white trillium, the painted trillium was quite rare in Ohio, and when I lived there I spent a lot of time hunting for even one. I was delighted to find many of these lovely flowers in Maine. They are common in North New Portland, Kingfield and in Baxter State Park. I have a note in my flower book that I found them growing profusely around Kidney Pond on May 20th, 1978 and again on the 22nd in 1980.

The description of the white trillium also fits the painted. However, the three white petals have a V-shaped splash of deep pink or red on them.

Henry David Thoreau exclaimed over the beautiful wild flowers he saw when he crossed Northeast Carry from Moosehead Lake to the West Branch of the Penobscot River in 1847. Among the flowers he mentioned were the painted trilliums, which still grow in that area.

Lady's Slipper or Moccasin-flower

Maine has many native orchids, and none are prettier than the lady's slipper. It grows about eight to twelve inches high, has two long oval leaves growing from the base of the stalk, and carries one blossom at the top. The color ranges from pale pink to red.

Mrs. Dana's book *How to Know the Wild Flowers* has a description of this flower which I like:

> *Graceful and tall the slender, drooping stem,*
> *With two broad leaves below,*
> *Shapely the flower so lightly poised between,*
> *And warm her rosy glow.*

And she goes on:

"The moccasin-flower is a blossom whose charm never wanes. It seems to be touched with the spirit of the deep woods, and there is a certain fitness in its Indian name, for it looks as though it came direct from the home of the red man."

One of my favorite lady's slippers is the pure white one. Its pedigree is a bit mixed, however. One authority calls it an albino. Roger Tory Peterson calls it "moccasin flower" (white form) and adds, "The white form is rare and local." Its Latin name is the same as for the pink, *Cypripedium acaule*.

Fannie Hardy Eckstorm has a charming story about this flower in her book *The Penobscot Man* in which she depicts this lady's slipper as "a coy blossom, a wanton, wayward flower who spreads her skirts and flutters her ribbons, curtseying and coquetting, and then hides herself in the forest, turns invisible, and every year seeks a new home.

"These were the demurest little flowers, not blushing pink like their coquettish sisters, but immaculately white and as staid as Quakeresses; there were eleven blossoms, a very large family for their tribe, and there was never a prettier bunch of lady's slippers."

Lady's slippers vary in color from white to pale pink to red. I have found the deeper colors in shady locations further back into the woods. They make a striking sight among the trees and often grow in large patches.

Yellow Lady's Slipper (Cypripedium calceolus)

The yellow lady's slipper, while quite common fifty years ago, has become quite rare. When I was young I knew where to find these pretty slippers in abundance on the edges of woods around Madison in Somerset County. A few years ago a cousin and I went searching in some of these remembered spots in Madison, Anson, and Industry, but came home disappointed. We didn't find one, and many of the farms which we knew as busy places were deserted. Oh, we found flowers, wild roses trailed over the old fences, and daisies and fireweed disguised the old cellar holes. But the lovely yellow lady's slipper had departed along with the farms' inhabitants.

Fortunately, they may be introduced into a wild flower garden successfully. I have only two small plants, but a naturalist friend has a beautiful large clump in her white pine woods where I went to photograph the ones in this picture.

Ram's-head Lady's Slipper

If you have never seen this flower, do not be surprised. They are quite rare in Maine, and in fact are quite rare anywhere and difficult to transplant as I can testify. I had three plants in my wild flower garden which were doing very well until two of them were chewed up by my family of chipmunks who live in the stone wall near the garden. I have put up a little fence around the third and only surviving plant and hope for the best. Next spring I will watch it (and the chipmunks) carefully.

The ram's-head, in contrast to the pink lady's slipper, has three or four wide veined leaves climbing up the stem, which is from six to twelve inches in height. Two of the petals are narrow and brown and could be likened to shoelaces above the slipper. The slipper pouch forms the third petal, which is white, veined with deep rose or red. Marilyn Dwelley in *Spring Wildflowers of New England* writes that this flower got its name from the elongated tip of the pouch which gives the ram's-head look to the blossom.

This flower is one of the smaller lady's slippers, being about one-third the size of the pink one.

Showy Lady's Slipper

This flower is one of our most beautiful native orchids and it is well-named, as it certainly is showy. The botanical name is equally appropriate as *Cypripedium reginae* means "slipper fit for a Queen."

It blooms in my wild flower garden near the Maine shore early in July after all my pink lady's slippers have gone by. I transplanted three small plants a few years ago and they have multiplied. Last year I counted seven blooms on one clump, and this year there were thirteen, a beautiful sight which necessitated inviting my flower-loving friends over for a look.

Roger Tory Peterson calls it our largest and most beautiful northern orchid.

Calypso Bulbosa (Fairy Slipper, Deer Head Orchid)

According to an old Greek myth, Calypso, the daughter of the great god Atlas who carried the heavens on his shoulders, lived all her life on the isolated island of Ortygia. Odysseus, famous traveler of the ancient world, is supposed to have lived with the seductive nymph Calypso on her island for seven years, until he finally tired of her and returned to his wife Penelope.

Leaving Greek legends aside, we find this lovely orchid growing in deep coniferous woods among beds of moss. The flower is similar in shape to the lady's slipper. Sepals and side petals are light purple, and the lip or toe of the slipper is splashed with purple spots.

The calypso, although fairly rare, grows in five Maine counties: Aroostook (on lands owned by the Nature Conservancy), Penobscot, Piscataquis, Kennebec and Somerset. Its blooming period ranges from May to July. I haven't as yet tracked one down in Maine at the right time for a photograph, but was lucky enough to make a spring visit to Washington state when they were in full bloom. My granddaughter, an amateur botanist, asked me to go out into their woods to identify what she called "deer head lady's slippers." I did, and was amazed and delighted to see the delicately beautiful calypso growing profusely among the trees on a mossy forest floor. It was a thrilling sight. We both sat right down on a nice soft patch of moss, she to sketch for a lovely flower watercolor, and I to set up my tripod for pictures.

BIRD MIGRATION

With the coming of spring, another one of nature's miracles takes place.

The bird migration is on. What instinct induces them to take flight by the thousands, even millions? And how they find the same location, year after year, and even more amazing, the same nesting places, is a mystery!

Rachel Carson has given us a graphic description of a bird migration. As seen through her perceptive eyes, this event takes on new significance and beauty.
She wrote:

> About midnight the flight began. The first flock of some threescore birds rose into the air, circled over the plain, and straightening out into flight formation headed south and east. Another and another flock found its wings and hurtled after the leaders, flying low over the tundra that rolled like a deep purple sea beneath them. There was strength and grace and beauty in every stroke of the pointed wings; there was power without end for the journey.
>
> *Under the Sea Wind,* p. 72

> They would be seen by men in boats far at sea, flying in a swift, straight course low to the water, like those who know their destination and suffer nothing to deter them. . . . In them burned once more the fever of migration, consuming with its fires all other desires and passions.

> But soon there would come a day when again the flocks would spring into the air, this time to head southward into the misty horizon where sky met sea. Southward they would lay their course across more than two thousand miles of ocean from Nova Scotia to South America.
>
> *Under the Sea Wind,* p. 74

Snowy Egret in Flight

Gulls in Flight

Gannetts' Courting Dance

Gannetts have white heads except in the mating season when they are buff.

Sandpipers and Gull

Little Green Heron

A Pair of Wood Ducks in an East Boothbay Pond

Many ospreys summer in Maine and in the Boothbay region, building their nests near the shore in pine trees or even on handy navigation markers. If you take Captain Bob Fish's sightseeing boat out of Boothbay Harbor, he will point out several of these nests in busy Townsend Gut and other locations. Another nest is on Fort Island just north of East Boothbay in a tall tree.

The osprey is an eagle-like hawk, blackish above and white below. It can hover with beating wings and dive feet first into the water to catch fish.

Ospreys are great builders, and even after the nest looks finished, the birds keep remodeling and enlarging it. Here father is bringing a twig for mother to work into the sides.

But it appears that she was not satisfied with its size, so he came back with a good long one.

American Bittern (Thunder Pumper or Stake Driver)

There is a pond that lies under a hill, where the threading roots of many trees — mountain ash, hickory, chestnut, oak and hemlock — hold the rains in a deep sponge of humus. The pond is fed by two streams that carry the runoff of higher ground to the west, coming down over rocky beds grooved in the hill. . . . Willows grow in the wet ground along the eastern shore of the pond where the overflow seeps down a grass-lined spillway, seeking its passage to the sea.

. . . The pond is called Bittern Pond, because never a spring passes without a few of these shy herons nesting in the bordering reeds, and the strange pumping cries of the birds that stand and sway in the cattails, hidden in the blend of lights and shadows, are thought by some who hear them to be the voice of an unseen spirit of the pond.

From Bittern Pond to the sea is two hundred miles as a fish swims.

Rachel Carson, *Under the Sea Wind*, pp. 221-212

Where Rachel Carson's Bittern Pond is is a mystery to me, although I've tried to guess. However, I have found my own Bittern Pond which actually answers her description quite well, including the bitterns which live in the reed-bordered outlet stream on the east shore of the pond. It is Kidney Pond in Baxter State Park. As Rachel Carson wrote, these birds are very shy and are aided in hiding by their coloring which is so like the color of the grasses they like to stay in that they have a natural camouflage.

The bird is most often seen with its head uplifted as though listening intently, and its plumage is striped in shades of beige and brown.

My husband and I have paddled our canoe, as quietly as possible, near the outlet of my Bittern Pond trying to catch sight of and photograph this interesting bird. Many times the silence has been broken by a loud *oong-KA-chonk, oong-KA-chonk, oong-KA-chonk* (which could be likened to the sound of a stake being driven into the ground) coming from the thick grasses which grow in the shallow water bordering the outlet stream.

After making all that racket to lure us on, the wily bittern does a disappearing act, so it is very difficult to get a photograph. This accounts for the fact the the few pictures I have of this bird were taken through a grassy shield!

Naturally I prize my bittern pictures because of the difficulty of the chase, especially *Bittern with a fish* and *Bittern with head pointed toward the sky as though listening intently*, which is the most characteristic pose of the American bittern.

Great Blue Heron

The large and handsome great blue heron frequents the lakes, ponds and salt marshes of Maine in the summer and migrates to Florida in the winter. The tall, bluish-gray bird makes a striking picture as he wades slowly in the shallow water searching for food. They primarily eat fish and frogs, and it is surprising how far this bird can stretch its neck to catch a fish, and how swiftly. A pair likes our small sheltered cove on the Damariscotta River, and we enjoy watching them fish from the rocks or even from the end of our dock. We discovered their nest in a tree barely a quarter mile down the shore. When they fly off, the neck is folded but the legs are stretched out straight behind them.

Bald Eagle

Damariscotta Lake's famous first family has done it again! Within easy sight of a minor road, ogled daily by motorists, walkers, and canoeists, viewed studiously through binoculars by birders and photographed by amateurs with simple cameras and by experts with sophisticated equipment, the pair of bald eagles which for many years has claimed the same area near Damariscotta Mills for its nesting territory is raising a single eaglet.

On Sunday, June 27th John and I brought some Pennsylvania friends to see this nest. The bulky structure, high in a white pine tree, was clearly visible from where we stood. It appeared empty but soon the lone, brown plumaged occupant stretched a wing and changed its position. Then we noticed an adult bald eagle, a silhouette in that light, perched motionless on a dead branch of another pine. Adult bald eagles are identical in appearance; we assumed the parent keeping vigil was the male.

Then the other parent, the female we'll say, flew in, circled the area, her broad dark wings out flat. The sun caught the bright white tail and head — a beautiful, thrilling sight. She alighted on the nest, solicitously checked on the youngster and then offered food. What a marvelous performance to witness!

These eagles do not "go south for the winter," but they do roam beyond their claimed territory after the fledglings can cope for themselves.

On June 21st (the day after National Bald Eagle Day which observed the 200th anniversary of Congress's adoption of the bald eagle as our national symbol) the lone nestling was banded by the Fish and Wildlife Service.

Bald eagles in Maine are not out of danger. The production level is not enough to maintain a stable population, but there has been definite improvement in recent years and this Damariscotta Lake nest is one of our most productive.

By Florence Heyl
Excerpted from "You Can Find It Wild"
July 8, 1982

Herring Gulls

It seems incredible now, when the herring gull seems to be the most common water bird along our shores that at one time its numbers in eastern North America were reduced to just one colony on the entire Atlantic Coast. This depletion was a direct result of the craze, in the late 1800's and early 1900's, for plumes and feathers for millinery adornment. The egrets and other plume birds were the first to be protected and so gulls and terns were the next victims. The Weeks-McLean Act, passed in 1913, was not the first attempt at protection of migratory birds but it was the first effective federal law. Theodore Roosevelt, president 1901-1909, had forwarded the cause of conservation, John Muir and John Burroughs had been writing with persuasive impact in behalf of persecuted wildlife, and the "National Association of Audubon Societies for the Protection of Wild Birds and Animals," incorporated in 1905, was gaining public support. It became embarrassing, rather than popular, to wear a hat decorated with a plume or wing or tail — just as it is embarrassing, today, to wear an ocelot or a leopard coat.

In a book published in 1917, although the herring gull is referred to as the most abundant gull of the Atlantic Coast, the species' breeding range is given with Maine for its southernmost limit. In 1925 another book states that they then nested as far south as Massachusetts. "Probably the herring gull once nested on small islands all along the coast of New England; but many years ago most nesting seabirds were driven away from our coasts by continued persecution, and it is only within recent years since protection has had some effect that they have begun to come back." (Edward Howe Forbush). In 1934 Richard Pough gives the herring gulls' breeding range as south to northern New Jersey. But the most recently published guide, *The Audubon Society Field Guide,* published in 1977, states that the herring gull now breeds south to the Carolinas.

We hear and see the herring gulls every day. They are part of our life here in Maine. As they soar over the ocean they are beautiful; as one drops a clam onto a ledge and then retrieves the tasty morsel we admire the bird's intelligence. But when we see them *en masse* at a dump we find the sight repulsive. Yet his willingness to scavenge, to eat our waste, should also command our admiration — and thanks. We must admire the bird for his adaptability. Our own pursuits have reduced the quantity of small fish and mollusks available to the gulls. So they follow the fishing boats in to shore and eat the discarded waste as it is tossed into the water. Our open dumps provide them with easy nourishment all winter long. At sea, the gulls flock where sewage and garbage is dumped. Its scavenging habits, although unpleasant to witness, are of very definite value to humans. If our own disposal methods remained unchanged and yet all the gulls were gone, we'd soon realize their service.

I salute the herring gulls. They are intelligent, adaptable birds whose niche in this world is a direct help to us.

And they are so very beautiful!

By Florence Heyl
Excerpted from "You Can Find It Wild"
July 5, 1979

Gull in Flight

Atlantic Puffins

The summer of 1981 marked the exciting and successful climax of a nine-year project, the purpose of which was to reestablish a breeding colony of Atlantic puffins on Eastern Egg Rock in Muscongus Bay.

Puffins have a peculiar life history. The nest is a burrow or rock cavity into which the parents carry small fish to the single chick until one night, about six weeks after hatching, the young bird leaves the burrow and, quite alone, proceeds directly to the open sea, never having seen its home island in daylight.

After two years at sea (no one knows where), guided by mysterious and unerring instinct, those young puffins that have survived return to that or at least a nearby island. They do not breed, however, until they are four or five years of age.

The reestablishment project, conceived and directed by Dr. Stephen Kress of Cornell University and sponsored by National and Maine Audubon Societies, involved bringing very young puffin chicks from burrows on Great Island, Newfoundland, placing them in man-made burrows on Eastern Egg Rock, feeding them small fish — and waiting! Many miles, many hours, much discomfort and infinite patience were required.

Dr. Kress and his team were jubilant when, on July 4, 1981, an adult puffin was first observed carrying fish into a natural, deep rock crevice and soon emerging without the fish. In all, nine pairs of Atlantic puffins bred on Eastern Egg Rock in 1981, their leg-bands identifying at least one of each pair as a transferred bird. A young puffin successfully fledged from each of the nine nests.

After one hundred years of absence, due to excessive hunting and egging a century ago, and after nine years of working toward this goal, Atlantic puffins were once again breeding at Eastern Egg Rock.

By Florence Heyl
Excerpted from "You Can Find It Wild"
July 30, 1981

Two Atlantic Puffins on the rocks on Machias Seal Island
Photograph by Madelaine Tetinek

Puffin just landing on the rocks on Machias Seal Island with a beak full of fish.
Photograph by Madelaine Tetinek

Great Egret

The great egret was formerly known as the American egret, the common egret, the large egret, the great white egret and the great white heron. It may be seen in Maine in the salt water lagoons reaching back into the salt marshes along the Atlantic shore. They are not often found on rocky shores as they like shallow water for wading and fishing.

It is a large bird with snowy white plumage which almost led to its extinction during the craze for hat plumes around the turn of the century. We are glad to report that ladies no longer wear plumes on their hats, nor do they even wear hats.

This magnificent bird feeds alone, patiently stalking fish, frogs and crayfish in shallow water along the shore. It is distinguished by its pure white feathers, yellow bill and black legs and feet.

Snowy Egret

The beautiful snowy egret, while not common in Maine, has been sighted in large numbers in ponds on Westport Island and in the Boothbay area. Roger Tory Peterson calls this little charmer "the heron with the golden slippers."

This little fellow appears as though he came north much too soon and is huddled up on the water's edge.

This little bird has fluffy feathers on its head and tail which made lovely plumes for hats — when women wore hats. Due to this the snowy egret, as well as the great egret, was almost exterminated around the turn of the century.

Little Snowy, to give it its nickname, may look a white angel but likes a good fight if another bird approaches a favorite perch too closely. This interloper turned tail in a hurry!

Now all is quiet on the pond with Little Snowy perfectly reflected in the still water.

Summer brings a promise all her own. The early spring flowers have fulfilled their destiny and now lie dormant until next spring's rebirth.

Birds have migrated and are now settled in their summer homes.

Trees have leafed out and are in their prime, casting welcome shade from the hot summer sun. In the forest it is shadowy and cool as the sun can barely penetrate the dense canopy of dark green leaves.

The water in the ponds and lakes warms up enough for the children to visit "the old swimming hole" where perhaps there is a supple birch to swing from, ending with a ducking.

Nature celebrates by bringing forth a whole new set of flowers more exotic, more colorful, and usually larger than the spring flowers just past.

As the scene changes day by day, flowers begin to blossom in the meadows, moving away from the woods and damp hollows. We can enjoy summer's display without walking down a wet path. The flowers will grow to the very edges of the road, making a beautiful and colorful border if the town's road machines have not been by.

Labrador Tea

This is a small woody shrub with a handsome cluster of white flowers at the ends of the branches. An easy way to identify this flower is to look for the velvety brown lining on the underside of the leaves. The Indians and pioneers prized this plant for the delicious tea they made with it.

Rhodora (Rhododendron canadense)

I saw a field of these on a drive to Newagen. First a few and then hundreds of the beautiful cerise flowers appeared along the roadside.

Ralph Waldo Emerson has described the rhodora beautifully in his poem, *The Rhodora.*

On being asked, whence is the flower?

In May, when sea-winds pierced our solitudes,
I found the fresh Rhodora in the woods,
Spreading its leafless blooms in a damp nook,
To please the desert and the sluggish brook.
The purple petals, fallen in the pool,
Made the black water with their beauty gay;
Here might the redbird come his plumes to cool,
And court the flower that cheapens his array.
Rhodora! if the sages ask thee why
This charm is wasted on the earth and sky,
Tell them dear, that if eyes were made for seeing,
Then beauty is its own excuse for being:
Why thou wert there, O rival of the rose!
I never thought to ask, I never knew:
But in my simple ignorance, suppose
The self-same power that brought me there
*   brought you.*

It has a delicate blossom with three lobes above and two below, and to complete the fragile effect, there are many curving, pinkish-purple stamens extending from the flower's center.

Fringed Polygala

Flowering wintergreen, bird-on-the-wing, or polygala — take your choice. I first spied this flower on the road to Kennebec Point one day, and from the car thought they were violets. However, the vivid pink coloring made me get out and go closer. Marilyn Dwelley says of it:

> Both leaves and flowers are clustered together at the top of the stem. The pink or magenta tube-like flower is made up of two pink sepals which are wing-shaped and three small petals which join together to form a hollow tube. Part of the third petal is fringed. The leaves and flower are both about an inch long and the leaves are sharply pointed.

John Burroughs wrote of them:

> It is rather a shy flower not to be found in every wood — one day we went up and down looking for it and were about to give up when we suddenly came upon a gay company of them beside an old woods road!
> It was as though a flock of rose-purple butterflies had alighted there on the ground before us!

Fragrant White Water Lily — Lily Pond, Barter's Island

Beloved by artists, these exotic flowers grow in quiet pools where they sway gently on a carpet of green lily pads. The pure white lilies, *Nymphaea odorata*, are very fragrant; their name derives from Nympha, the Greek goddess of nature. Nymphs were lovely creatures associated with all natural things such as water, woods, meadows and gardens. The blooms are at the top of a long slender stem rising from rhyzomes which lie on the bottom of the pool.

Pink (Japanese) Water Lily — Appalachie Pond

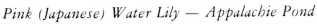

Ox Eye Daisy

What little girl has not searched out a quiet spot in a field away from prying eyes and played the little game "he loves me — he loves me not" with her heart falling a bit if the very last snow white petal says "he loves me not."

The focal point of the blossom is the large deep yellow center. In reality these are disk flowers, too numerous and too small to be seen individually unless magnified. The ray flowers are the white petals growing outward around the center.

The daisy is not native but was brought to our country by the early colonists, and we find it mentioned in the history of Dresden. It was growing in the neighborhood of the Pownalborough Courthouse in 1761.

Chaucer alludes to the name in the following:

That well by reason men call it may,
The Daisie, or else the eye of the day.

Chicory

Bluish-lavender, stalkless blossoms grow on a nearly bare stem. The petals are square-tipped and fringed; they completely close by noon or in the rain.

Yellow Hawkweed

Although called a weed, it is a very handsome flower and like the orange hawkweed is widespread.

Lupine

Our Maine lupine is an escaped garden flower which has become naturalized and beautifies many fields and roadsides with its rainbow of colors.

Black-eyed Susan

By the middle of July, meadow and roadside alike are a mass of sunny orange. Black-eyed Susans nod from every corner in company with yellow day lilies and deep mauve milkweed blossoms. What gorgeous color harmonies nature dreams up for our enjoyment.

These flowers were first brought from the American west mixed with clover seed. They spread rapidly, to the dismay of farmers but to the delight of flower lovers.

Butter and Eggs, Also Known As Toadflax

The flowers resemble snapdragons, and the leaves are feathery and slender. The blossoms grow along the stem forming a long spike and are of two shades of yellow.

Columbine

The columbine excites our imagination with its delicate beauty as it dances around on its slender stem in the merest breeze, never seeming to pause for a moment. It may look delicate, but its habitat is anything but that, as it prefers to sink its roots into gravelly soil or even around a stone wall. For this reason it is often called rock bell.

The lovely tiger lily has blossoms which hang downward, the backward curling petals of orange spotted with dark purple. It is an escapee from cultivation, now growing wild along dry roadsides or fields.

Day Lily

This lily faces upward and is a tawny orange color. It has clusters of long, narrow buds at the top of the stem which open for one day only, then fade to be replaced by another opening bud. The day lily is not a native wild flower, but is another escapee from cultivation.

87

Wood Lily

*"Even Solomon in all his glory
Was not arrayed like one of these."*

The familiar Biblical quotation certainly applies to this flower with its robes of brightest scarlet.

We always feel a sense of elation when we see here and there in the shadowy woods a vivid flash of color caused by the wood lily, two or three feet high with three to five blossoms with their faces toward the sky.

This plant is particularly luxuriant and bright near our Atlantic shoreline. This picture was taken in Reid State Park where the lily grows interspersed with pink roses forming a veritable mosaic of pink and red, an unforgettable sight.

*St. John's-wort
(Hypericum perforatum)*

St. John's-wort is named for St. John the Baptist. Its pretty yellow blossoms open on or near June 24th, which is the saint's festival day. Since the sun is high in the sky in late June, the plant is considered to be a chaser of darkness, gloom and the devil.

Young maidens believed that their marital future could be influenced or foretold by this flower, and they tended the plants carefully. If the plants thrived and had many blossoms, the coming year would bring wedding bells.

*The wonderful herb
whose leaf will decide
If the coming year will
make me a bride.*

Wild Calla Lily

I photographed this lovely white lily on Westport Island where there is a small pond with what seemed like acres of these lilies. Sometimes called water arum, it used to be common all over New England but is now quite rare.

New England Aster

Late summer brings the New England aster along with many other varieties. There are New York asters, New Hampshire asters, showy asters, etc. They range in color from a pale pinkish lavender to a striking deep purple.

In form and color this is the most regal of our wildflowers, so no wonder it was chosen by Louis VII as his personal emblem thus becoming the fleur-de-lis of France.

In spite of the fact that it is often called blue flag, the color is really a deep purple, and it is often seen on our Maine roads in June, being showy enough to be spotted even from a car moving at medium speed.

I have seen beautiful patches of this wild iris beside the road between Norridgewock and Augusta, also near Belgrade and close to the shore in marshy spots at Ocean Point in Boothbay.

Cardinal Flower

A slender spike of intense scarlet blossoms, Mrs. Dana wrote of it: "We have no flower which can vie with this in vivid coloring. In late summer, its brilliant red gleams from the marshes or is reflected from the shadowy water's edge with unequalled intensity."

As if some wounded eagle's breast
Slow throbbing o'er the plain,
Had left its airy path impressed
In drops of scarlet rain.

Holmes

Early French Canadian settlers admired the flower so much they sent it to France, where it was given the name cardinal flower for its resemblance to the brilliant red robes of cardinals.

90

The purple fringed orchis is amazingly beautiful. Not feeling equal to the task of doing it justice, I went to my favorite flower book *How to Know the Wild Flowers* by Mrs. Dana only to find out that she had passed the buck to Henry David Thoreau! He wrote:

I found the Great Fringed Orchis . . . a large spike of peculiarly delicate pale purple flowers growing in the luxuriant and shady swamp amid the ferns! It is a beauty reared in the shade of a convent, who never strayed beyond the sound of the convent bell!

To A Fringed Gentian
By William Cullen Bryant

Thou blossom bright with autumn dew,
And colored with the heaven's own blue,
That openest when the quiet light
Succeeds the keen and frosty night,

Thou comest not when violets lean
O'er wandering brooks and springs unseen,
Or Columbines, in purple dressed,
Nod o'er the ground-bird's hidden nest.

Thou waitest late and com'st alone,
When woods are bare and birds are flown,
And frosts and shortening days portend
The aged year is near his end.

Then doth thy sweet and quiet eye
Look through its fringes to the sky,
Blue — blue — as if that sky let fall
A flower from its cerulean wall.

I would that thus, when I shall see
The hour of death draw near to me,
Hope, blossoming within my heart,
May look to heaven as I depart.

Bluest of all blue flowers and most treasured find of an autumn walk is the fringed gentian. It blooms in September and October along Maine's rural roadsides and in unmown meadows. Standing about a foot high, with four rounded, fringed petals flaring out from a bell-shaped tube, this lovely blue, blue flower, *Gentiana crinita,* is becoming more and more rare and is already extinct in many areas where it was once common.

Here in Maine we've found fringed gentians blooming in several places: in roadside ditches, in open meadows, even in a hayfield, owned by people who appreciate wild flowers. They mow early in the season, before these late bloomers would have made their upward thrust.

Locations of fringed gentian "stations" are usually well guarded secrets, shared only with friends who can be trusted, like Edna St. Vincent Millay, to "touch a hundred flowers and not pick one."

The fringed gentian is a biennial plant. If a seed is blown or dropped to a suitable environment, it will have a good chance of producing a flowering plant two years later.

By Florence Heyl
Excerpted from "You Can Find It Wild"

Too soon there comes a day that signals the end of summer. Suddenly the wind shifts. The north wind over the forest has its first chill, and there is a snap to the air.

We know another season is on the way.

The long bright days of summer swiftly passed,
The dry leaves whirled in Autumn's rising blast,
And evening cloud and whitening sunrise rime
Told of the coming of the winter-time.

From "Bridal of Pennacook"
By John Greenleaf Whittier

AUTUMN

This is a good time to explore one of Maine's country roads, and fortunately there are still some left.

They are a challenge to me as I always wonder what could lie around the next bend. A pond? A shady nook? A pretty farm? A deer or moose? All are possible.

John Muir had this to say about the forests he loved so much.

The winds go to every tree;
fingering each leaf and branch,
and furrowed bole,
not one is forgotten.

The mountain pine
towering with outstretched arms
on the rugged buttresses of the icy peaks;
they seek and find them all,
caressing them tenderly.

Birches along the Carrabassett River near Kingfield

The visitor to the woods may not know pine from spruce, or cedar from fir, but he is sure to recognize the white birch, queen of Maine's trees.

A group of Dresden pupils follows Florence Heyl, nature writer, down the nature trail at Pownalborough Courthouse. This trail follows the bank of the Kennebec River for a distance and then returns to the courthouse through the woods.

What fun to walk along a woodland trail, shedding the cares of a busy day, to look for the secrets of the forest floor! So come along and tread lightly lest we crush some of nature's tiny masterpieces under our feet.

A small strawberry plant has somehow sprung up in the rocks next to a small mountain cataract.

Among the smallest of nature's miniatures is the matchstick lichen or British soldiers, barely one fourth of an inch tall. They grow among moss and other lichens. The little cup-shaped green ones are pixie cups.

Yellow Chaparelle is the name of these small mushrooms which spring up after a shower in the open woods.

And from every old stump and the earth around them clumps of color have emerged like this fly amanita in the brightest of yellows. They have a short life and in a day or two will start turning black.

Finding a perfect specimen is difficult, because small animals take large bites and pull them over. This luscious looking bunch of honey mushrooms won't last long!

After a good downpour I can often find the delicately lovely Indian pipes in my woods. These, like the other types of mushrooms and fungi, have sprung from decaying wood and vegetation.

A little poem by Mary Higgenson has caught the ethereal quality of these waxlike "pipes."

> In shining groups, each stem a pearly ray,
> Weird flecks of light within the shadowed woods.
> They dwell aloof, a spotless sisterhood.
> No Angelus, except the wild birds' lay, awakes these forest nuns!
> Yet night and day, their heads are bent,
> As if in prayerful mood!

There are small flowers to be found on the forest floor also. White wood sorrel has delicate tracings of pink on its petals, and leaves which look like four-leaf clovers. We found these at Enchanted Pond.

New life springing from old! Fungi, mosses and grass starting to beautify an old stump left behind by a logging crew many years ago.

Blow-downs and old, dead bleached trees add to the somber mood of a dense forest on the trail to Upper Enchanted Pond in Enchanted Township.

The best known trail in Maine is the Appalachian, which starts at the summit of Mount Katahdin and extends to Georgia, a distance of over two thousand miles. I have only hiked a few of those miles, and those were in Baxter State Park and in the Mount Bigelow region. These areas are perfectly beautiful and still quite unspoiled due, in Baxter State Park, to Governor Baxter's firm directive that "the park shall remain forever wild."

For those who like short hikes without any steep grades, the stretch between the park road to Daicey Pond, and then on to Big and Little Niagara Waterfalls, is a happy choice.

The trail is well marked with slashes of white paint on the trees at about eye height. The rule is if you don't see a white blaze, return to the one just past to reconnoiter. There should be a blazed tree in sight at all times.

This trail is
bordered with ferns
for much of the way.
Their soft green
color and feathery,
lacy fronds help to
make this an
outstanding and
delightful hike.

There are dense forests rising to the slopes of
Mount Katahdin, and continuing northward to the
Canadian border.

The Nesowadnehunk River is a rocky, fast flowing stream which enters the West Branch of the Penobscot River a few miles below the falls.

There is a half-mile stretch in this river which is said to drop four hundred feet. This stretch of fast water includes two waterfalls with continuous cascades between. First is Little Niagara.

Big Niagara Falls is situated in a beautiful wood with large, flat-topped ledges at the foot of the falls. These make a perfect grandstand from which to watch the magnificent fall of water over the sheer escarpment. The turbulent water seems to be heading straight for your ledge, when it is suddenly deflected and boils off down the channel.

What a perfect place for a picnic!

Or a cook-out with Junior York, our favorite Maine guide, presiding over the fire. Trout are on sticks in front of the fire (done to a turn when the eyes turn white), fried potatoes, onions prepared according to the guide's special recipe ("Cook hell out of them") and finally, steak done just right.

The Appalachian Trail winds its way westward from Baxter State Park. After passing north of Pleasant Pond, it makes its only bridgeless river crossing when it crosses the Kennebec River near Caratunk. This village is a food and mail stop for hikers, and there are also boats for rent.

Cathedral Pines, situated on the Dead River, was one of Arnold's camping spots and is now a popular picnic ground. Perhaps one of the largest groves of pine trees remaining in Maine, it is worth a visit.

The ascent of Mount Bigelow is started near this point. The trail leads across the twelve mile ridge of the Bigelow Range.

John and Florence Heyl canoeing on Kidney Pond, Baxter State Park

During the last Ice Age, a huge glacial drift from the Canadian highlands, a mile deep, pushed its way across Maine, cropping off mountain tops and scooping out valleys. It was then that our vast territory of interlacing streams, ponds and lakes came into being. Beginning with the Indians, who used waterways as highways, and extending to the present time, boating has enabled nature lovers to penetrate into the wilderness.

People who enjoy the Baxter State Park scenery and fishing are restricted to the use of canoes, as no motors are allowed on the wilderness lakes.

Fishing is the most popular sport at Kidney Pond in the park, although just paddling around the lake and outlet is a close second. The chances are very good that you will spot moose, loons, or even the shy American bittern.

Pitcher Plant or Huntsman's Cup

I found this unusual plant on a canoe trip on Rocky Pond in Baxter State Park. My friends tried valiantly to keep the canoe right side up, while I rummaged for my small tripod and camera. They succeeded, so I got my pictures without dunking the three of us!

The leaves of this plant have an odd pitcher-like shape. They are lined with a sugary material, below which they are smooth. Still lower there are stiff bristles pointing downward. Insects attracted by the sweet secretion find themselves unable to crawl out, a perfect insect trap.

Thoreau wrote of it:

> Though the moss is comparatively dry, I cannot walk without upsetting the numerous pitchers, which are now full of water and so wetting my feet. I accidentally sat down on a bunch of them and found an uncomfortably wet seat where I expected a dry one. I think we have no other plant so singular and remarkable.

The pitcher plant has a red or purple blossom in the early part of June.

Lily Pad Pond may be reached by paddling across Kidney Pond, hiking to Lily Pad, a little less than a mile, then setting out for a trip around Lily Pad Pond in one of the camp canoes. It is a pretty pond with views of Mount Katahdin, OJI, Double Top and Sentinel.

Mount Katahdin, Baxter State Park

Shore Path at Kidney Pond

View from Camden Hills State Park

From the summit of Mount Battie, one has a lovely view of the hills to the west and of the bay to the east. This is the spot which the young Edna St. Vincent Millay visited often. She was so moved by the surrounding scenery that she wrote one of her loveliest poems there. In "Renascence" she tells of looking one way to see three mountains, then in the other direction to see three islands in the bay.

It is certainly one of the most beautiful panoramas along the Maine coast.

Autumn Scene

All nature trails are not inland. Walks along the sea remind us that there are many fascinating plants and animal life to be found on the margins where the sea and land meet. I've noticed that flowers grow on the shore right in the salt spray and have especially brilliant colors. Lichens and mussels cling to the rocks, and the water itself has its own beauty, ever changing with the time of day and state of the weather. Watching the surf on a windy day is a favorite pastime, one wave after another, and another, and another.

Surf at Reid State Park

Boulder Reflections on the Damariscotta River

The Sound of the Sea
By Henry Wadsworth Longfellow

The Sea awoke at midnight from its sleep,
And round the pebbly beaches far and wide
I heard the first wave of the coming tide
Rush onward with uninterrupted sweep;
A voice out of the silence of the deep,
A sound mysteriously multiplied
As of a cataract from the mountain's side,
Or roar of winds upon a wooded steep.
So comes to us at times, from the unknown
And inaccessible solitudes of being,
The rushing of the sea-tides of the soul;
And inspirations, that we deem our own,
Are some divine foreshadowing and foreseeing
Of things beyond our reason or control.

Tide pools, those miniature seas, are fascinating. I love to try to capture their charm and contents on film.

Rachel Carson, who could find beauty in all aspects of nature, had the gift of describing what she saw. She wrote:

> Tide pools contain mysterious worlds within their depths, where all the beauty of the sea is subtly suggested and portrayed in miniature. Some of the pools occupy deep crevices or fissures; at their seaward ends these crevices disappear under water, but toward the land they run back slantingly into the cliffs and the walls rise higher, casting deep shadows over the water within them.
>
> *The Edge of the Sea (hardcover),* p. 110

> By day there are other moods. Some of the most beautiful pools lie high on the shore. Their beauty is the beauty of simple elements — color and form and reflection. I know one that is only a few inches deep, yet it holds all the depth of the sky within it, capturing and confining the reflected blue of far distances.
>
> p. 111

Queen Anne's Lace or Wild Carrot

Although Roger Tory Peterson gives the name "wild carrot" to this flower, I prefer the common name, Queen Anne's lace. This name is certainly descriptive of the pure white blossom which looks for all the world like a round medallion of the finest lace. Another name is "bird's nest," suggested by the way the old flower clusters curl into a cuplike shape.

Purple loosestrife is called long purple by English country people. It grows profusely along the shore at Ocean Point. The deep purple-pink flowers grow along the stem to form a striking spike.

The forest has a special quality just after a rain shower. The woods road glistens, pine needles are a deep chocolate brown, and the bark on the trees drips with raindrops!

Even the fallen leaves have an oilcloth-like finish with deep saturated colors. They shine and seem alive again. As they fall and drift around, they arrange themselves in an autumn mosaic.

Droplets cling to the ferns along the path, bending them a little towards the earth.

Moisture spreads to all the hidden nooks of the forest floor, dramatizing all the miniature blossoms just begging to be noticed. The exquisite goldthread is like a cluster of tiny jewels in a setting of green.

Mushroom in a Bed of Green

A summer cottage on Wyman Lake is completely wreathed in brilliant hues.

Trees
By Elizabeth Hamilton Hartsgrove

Just yesterday you looked so green and fair;
  Wee buds were breaking into leaf
And blossoms filled the air
  With fragrance sweet.

Today I passed again, and truly thought
  Your leaves were like a rainbow drawn;
The miracle was wrought
  Before the dawn.

Tomorrow winds will sweep away your crown;
  The year is past and life had fled;
Your leaves are old and brown
  And some are dead.

Somehow, earth wears its pattern like a tree;
  We live and love and die, but Spring
Comes after you and me
  With life again.

With a little imagination we find ourselves transported to an open air church, surrounded with beautiful blue and gold stained glass windows and with the whitest of columns before the door.

The greens are now subdued and become a minor color among a riot of reds, oranges and russets.

The birches lag behind the maples in turning color, but soon add their beautiful yellows to the scene.

A yellow wood casting its reflection on Kingsbury Lake, off Route 16 between Bingham and Abbot.

Golden days come in a long series, each like a gift which we clutch to our hearts and cherish.

The magic of October color lies in the way the sunlight filters through the leaves of gold and red.

The leaves reflect the light in all directions, diffusing it so that it seems to come not only from overhead, but from all sides and even from deep within the woods.

Nature, as though not quite satisfied with the real beauty on the shore of Kingsbury Lake, has given us a chance to enjoy it twice by reflecting everything in the still water.

These are the bittersweet days. As the wheel of time turns again, always surprising us a little, the golden days of autumn are almost over.

All at once, the impatient swish of the northeast wind can be heard on the hillsides.

The deer, half seen
are to covert wending . . . .

Sir Walter Scott

It descends and roars down the valley,

rustling the leaves with a sound like the taffeta skirts our grandmothers wore.

The gusts blow the leaves and small branches around briskly, warning us of the coming of winter.

And all too soon, one, then another and another leaf detaches itself and gently, gently drifts to the ground.

And that, my friends, marks the end of one more glorious autumn in the north woods of Maine.

A quiet pond with its gift of color gently wafted from the overhanging boughs.

We still linger to admire the beauty of a single branch.